What About Real Estate Investing?

A Realistic Guide for Individuals Wanting To Make Monthly Income And Profits From Real Estate

by

Karl Caswell

authorHOUSE
1663 LIBERTY DRIVE, SUITE 200
BLOOMINGTON, INDIANA 47403
(800) 839-8640
www.authorhouse.com

First published by AuthorHouse 02/03/05

ISBN: 1-4184-1215-5(e)
ISBN: 1-4184-1216-3 (sc)

Library of Congress Control Number: 2004090189

Printed in the United States of America
Bloomington, IN

This book is printed on acid free paper.

Thank you to:

Kristeen, Blake, and Cody for your love and encouragement.

Mom and Dad for your wisdom and steering me in the right direction.

Mr. Lee and Miss Pat for your lifelong friendship and being my second parents.

Shack, Lantz, Joel, Tommy, Greg, Steve, Duhon, Mike, Reggie, Jimbo, Moe, Kevin, Craig, Tim, Russ, Rusty, Michael, Joe, Curtis, Barry, Ray, Ricky, Mark, and Dad for the good times.

Paul, Keith, and Mr. Ray because your success has driven mine.

This is general information about real estate investing. Some statements are pertinent to certain areas of the country that may include yours. The advice should not be taken as legal advice and you should check with local, state and federal laws concerning investing in your area.

Table of Contents

***EVERYTHING SHOULD BE MADE AS
SIMPLE AS POSSIBLE, BUT NOT SIMPLER.***

ALBERT EINSTEIN

INTRODUCTION

Several years ago, I realized that average people in today's work force could obtain financial freedom. This work force is filled with people like you and me. Some are searching for the right direction in their financial lives to someday attain this financial freedom.

There are many ways one could begin to achieve financial success. I think owning real estate is one of the best investments America has to offer. It has been in the past, it is right now, and will be in the future. My father once said that people do not need money, they need income. We live in a monthly payment society. Many Americans can create a monthly income by investing in real estate.

I chose real estate investing ten years ago as a part-time business. It has become full time and now I work when I choose to. However, it wasn't easy. It took determination and sacrifice. I chose the conservative route because it fit my investing interest. My personal plan was well thought out years before investing took place and it was not accomplished overnight. I spent my time listening, reading, learning, and planning. It was a good place to start, a place where you can

2

now begin. It doesn't cost anything to learn and plan, so get in touch with your inner drive. You might find that you can accomplish some of these investment strategies much quicker than others. Time goes by quickly, so get started now! It has worked for me in small town America. I hope that you find these ideas can work for you also. Let's explore simple steps one might take. We will not do this with facts, figures, or economic matters of opinion, but with common sense approaches that may help you attain the level of success that is suitable for you.

I AM ONLY ONE, BUT STILL I AM ONE.
I CANNOT DO EVERYTHING, BUT STILL
I CAN DO SOMETHING AND BECAUSE
I CANNOT DO EVERTHING I WILL NOT
REFUSE TO DO THE SOMETHING THAT I
CAN DO.

EDWARD EVERETT HALE

CHAPTER 1

WHAT ABOUT DETERMINING YOUR PORTFOLIO POSITION?

Where are you now in today's fast forward electronic economy? Do you measure up? This depends on your definition of measuring up. You may want a different level of success than someone else. First you must define the type of success you want for yourself. Success for you is probably completely different than it is for me. You, and you alone, must determine what it is. Many people have a lifelong desire for attaining money and wealth. Without this achievement they might consider themselves unsuccessful. Others might achieve success in other areas. For example, they may be passionate about their families. Watching their children grow and become assets to our society may make them feel successful.

I saw my grandmother as a very successful person. She got married at the early age of thirteen. Her first husband was killed in a boating accident. It was not customary for a girl to go back to her parents after marrying. Therefore, she married again at the age of fourteen to a man with seven children.

She went on to have six children with my grandfather. He also died at an early age while she was pregnant with her last child. Needless to say, in the late fifties and early sixties, she had a very tough time with that many children to take care of alone. Throughout this trying time of her life, she never had extra money. However, remember success is an individual accomplishment. In my opinion, she was very successful. She cared for and loved her children and grandchildren throughout her life. She loved to get together with people and share stories and always loved family reunions. Her influence is still evident in the family she left behind. She was truly successful, not financially, but in other ways.

DEFINE SUCCESS FOR YOU

Anyone can find success. I strive for success in all areas of life including my financial life. Set your personal goals and reach for them. Again, determine the level you are at now, and where you want to be in the future. Write your goals down in the back of this book and review them from time to time. This will help you to have specific targets to work toward. There is a lot of merit to putting your goals in writing. It can and will help you to strive for them. Make these goals something you have to do, not just something you want to do. Be specific about your goals in a realistic time frame. This will give you a sense of accomplishment as you begin to achieve them.

A wonderful thing about real estate investing is that it is never too late to start. If you begin in the early working years of your life, you can create yourself a sizeable monthly income and net worth. Once you accomplish your goals you can then create income for your children or loved ones. You can also get the ball rolling in the later stages of your life. You can create a monthly income from real estate that can be used for future tuition costs, luxury items, or vacations.

Where were you when you realized that more money was needed to maintain the lifestyle that you had with your parents or grandparents? Life suddenly begins when the utility bills are your sole responsibility. These have been frightening moments for most of us. These moments might have sparked thoughts of hard work to obtain what we want. Once you have reached this stage of your life, the question can be asked, "What have you done with the fruits of your hard work?" Take a moment to reflect upon the early decisions that you have made or are making at this moment. Are you looking in the past and thinking 'those were the good ole days'? Guess what! You are living the good ole days right now!

So what is success for you? It's an individual thing. Determine your personal goal and where you want to be at different stages of your life. You may be fifteen or seventy years of age. At fifteen, you may be building for your future. At seventy, you can build for the future of your loved ones. The key word is to begin. You must start something now so that you can have later. Make your first goal lead to the next so you will feel a sense of accomplishment as you go. Do this! Position your thoughts and actions to obtain the goals that you will set for yourself. Only you know what you want in life. Your goals will be the engine that will drive your actions.

I was twenty-seven years old when I did this. I didn't have even one investment property, but I wanted many. I knew that just wanting them would not get me there. So I thought about what I had done so far. My goal was to have ten houses in eight years. I did not think this was out of my reach and it wasn't. It was a realistic goal for me. This helped me to get well on my way to living my life the way I wanted it to be. I didn't want someone else to dictate my life and time. Think about yourself now. You might be excited about your accomplishments thus far. If so, that is great. You are on the right track. If not, this might be the time to begin your journey of real estate investing. Make careful observations about your current position and where you want to be in order to attain the level of success you want for yourself.

We all have the same amount of time in every day. Consequently, why do you work? Are you getting the most out of your allotted time? Are you giving yourself quiet time and your family valuable time? A lot of people today find themselves worn out at the end of the day. The physical and mental strain from their everyday jobs can be very tiring. I'm sure it is hard to juggle your time between your job, kids, spouse, household duties, family, friends, and then yourself. Some people have to work sixty hours a week or more. Do you find yourself here? Are you working this much because of a great reward in the future? If you are working this much, but sacrifice the things you love in the process, is it worth it in the end? What do you have to show for your long hours of work thus far? Try to put yourself in a frame of mind that would allow you time for yourself and family, while accomplishing your goals. Do you think people would like to work less if they were given that choice? I'm sure everyone would answer yes to that question. This might be the time in your life to take steps that will enable you to work less in the future. You must sacrifice now to have later. There is no better time than now. If you are already on your way, keep striving.

SACRIFICE NOW
TO HAVE LATER

I know everyone wants more leisure time. We would like more time to free our minds from the everyday grind of work, bills, household tasks, and everyday problems. But it is hard to find time for leisure activities. A career in real estate investing can offer these benefits. Once you decide to exert the effort to create this new business for yourself, you have then taken the first step toward having more free time in the future. Control your own destiny. Write on your goal sheet how much income it would take to achieve your goals. This is what I call a base income, an income that can fund your monthly bills so that you can concentrate on real estate investing and not an 8 to 5 job for the next 20 or 30 years. Income from six houses drastically reduced my work hours. My income remained the same, but my time spent working was less. This created more free time for me to devote to my real estate investing business. This free time enabled me to find more properties and create more deals. Each new deal increased my income and my free time. As you can see, it became easier with each step. It takes time initially to find, purchase, and repair a property, but the benefit of this short amount of time is enormous. Your reward is income for years into the future. Real estate investing can do this for you! It can help you set your own hours of the day. Because your time can be flexible, your days could become less stressful. This flexibility might allow you to move forward with a clear decisive way of managing your business.

Find your stress reliever, something that you can enjoy while planning your future. Golf, tennis, basketball, football, baseball, hiking, camping, or fishing can be very fun and they might give you time to reflect upon your goals and accomplishments. Family time and mini-vacations are also stress relievers. Again, real estate investing can do this for you. It can provide you with an income while you are playing, working on another job, or even while you are sleeping. Try taking a few steps now so you can be rewarded in the future.

If you are currently in a job, try finding ways to increase your income in order to invest. Try to pay yourself a percentage of your income strictly to invest. Do this consistently to have money in position to invest when the time arrives. If there is no extra income, try a different job or a second job. I've done this for years. I've taken money from part-time jobs and used the income strictly to invest in long-term investments. Remember, you must sacrifice now to have later. My wife and I sacrificed for ten years by not taking vacations or buying luxury items, but now we have the rest of our lives to enjoy the benefits of these sacrifices. You might be able to accomplish your goals even quicker. The key is to begin. Time flies, so take steps to start now.

No matter what financial position you find yourself in, you can start a real estate investing business. It must be a determined, decisive choice that you make. You can begin right now by organizing your thoughts and plans. Write your goals down. That is one of the most important steps. You will know where you are and where you want to be. Planning now will allow you to create a business plan that can and will guide you. When you find and purchase your first investment property, you will be prepared to repair, rent, or sell the property. Start thinking and planning for your first property. Once you do the first one, I think you will see the opportunity that awaits you.

During the course of this book, I will share some real estate investing ideas and examples that have helped me. I hope some of these investing ideas will help you. Just one idea or many might spark interest in your new business—your very own real estate investing business. Start now by:

- Determining your portfolio position. If you have no portfolio, start one.
- Determining the level of success you want for yourself.
- Writing specific goals down and reviewing them.
- Devising ways to control your time.
- Finding ways to have extra money to invest.
- Beginning your real estate investing business.

IN THE LONG RUN, MEN HIT ONLY WHAT
THEY AIM AT.

HENRY DAVID THOREAU

CHAPTER 2

WHAT ABOUT A GOOD FOUNDATION?

Some investors may not agree that a great place to start investing is in smaller, less expensive properties. I believe it is better because of the ease of getting started. In most cases, smaller homes are more suited for building a good base income. It is easier to purchase houses for twenty five to thirty five thousand dollars than it is to purchase houses for one hundred thousand. It is also quicker to pay off. Would you agree it would be much easier and faster to pay off thirty thousand than it would be to pay off one hundred thousand with rents and extra income? Less expensive properties usually stay rented also. The pool of people who rent less expensive homes is greater. I'll bet in most areas people want to rent for five to eight hundred dollars not twelve to fifteen hundred. Most people that want to pay the larger amounts want to buy, not rent. There are both, but try to target the biggest pool of renters in your area. The rents in larger cities might be much more expensive than smaller cities and towns. The figures I am using are relevant to the part of the country I live in. Your area may be different than mine so find the target rent in your area. This will help you know the price range of investment houses to purchase. Metropolitan areas are more expensive, but incomes are greater also. It is all relative to the area you are living in. Your positive cash flow will increase quicker with the less expensive properties because they will be paid off sooner. Then you can use the income from one to pay for two, then two incomes paying for the third and so on. For instance, if house one, two, and three rent for $500 each and house one and two are paid for, the third house can be paid for much quicker. Let's assume house three has a $30,000 mortgage:

HOUSE 1	$ 500 monthly
HOUSE 2	$ 500 monthly
HOUSE 3	$ 500 monthly
TOTAL	$1,500 monthly income

The bank note on a $30,000 mortgage for 30 years at a rate of 7% would be approximately $200. Therefore, an extra $1,300 can be used to buy the mortgage down. Keep your notes low on investment property by getting 30-year loans in case of cash flow problems and be sure the loan has no pre-payment penalties. The third house could be paid for in approximately two years. Now you are on your way to the fourth with even more positive cash flow that will enable you to pay for it quicker. I think you understand that the seventh house will be paid for much quicker than the third by combining all incomes to buy the mortgage down.

You need to determine how much you want your base income to be and how long it will take you to get there. I think having positive cash flow quickly is a great way to start a real estate investing business. Not only do you have the asset of the properties you purchase, but you also have the income to help you to purchase additional properties. Therefore, your business continues to grow. At some point, if you choose to purchase houses that range from $100,000-$150,000, wouldn't it be great to have an income base from smaller properties helping pay for the larger ones? It would be scary for most if a house and mortgage that cost $120,000 became vacant. Where would you get the $1,200 for the note? Maybe this would be easy for some, but not for most beginning investors. Having a good foundation of income from less expensive properties will make it much less stressful to purchase more expensive ones. Use the income from properties with no debt to acquire better investments. You do not have to keep a less expensive property long-term, just allow the income from it to help you build your business for long-term investments.

I once purchased a property that was owner financed with no money down. My note was $200 monthly, but the income was $700 monthly. The purchase price was $15,000. It was a real bargain because the original owner wanted out of the property. I did nothing to this property, but collect money. It was not in a very good area, but I used the investment as a stepping-stone to other more desirable properties. With creative financing, I was able to pay for this property in full within the first year. Once the property was paid for, I was able to owner finance it to someone else. I became the bank. Payments were deposited into my bank account monthly for about two more years. My equity in this property was needed to purchase a house in a better area, so I contacted a mortgage broker. A mortgage broker acts as a middleman between you and lending institutions. They broker the mortgage for you to financial institutions. I held a note for $27,000. The mortgage broker found a bank that wanted to purchase the note from me. An institution must discount notes somewhat to make the deal attractive enough for their investment. They offered me $23,000. Good for me, good for them. Good for me because I was able to use cash from this property as a stepping-stone to a better one. Good for the bank because they now own a $27,000 note at 10% interest for just $23,0000. With the rents and increased value of the property, my profit was about $18,000. Remember, I did nothing to this property but collect money. At that time of my life it would have taken me a while to just save $18,000 from extra income. Even though it was in a bad area, it worked at the time. It was a short-term investment that propelled me into a long-term investment.

DON'T OVERLOOK LESS DESIRABLE PROPERTIES

Less expensive properties in non-desirable neighborhoods should not be overlooked. However, choose the neighborhood wisely. Don't purchase properties where property values are diminishing because crime rates may be rising in that area. Also, people may be beginning to take less pride in their homes and allowing them to devalue. Search for the bargains. If you choose to purchase a house in an older, less expensive neighborhood, make sure the area is improving or at least holding it's own. Making improvements to your investment might spark others to do the same. You may not choose to hold this type of house as a long-term investment, but it could be used for short-term profits. Quick cash from these properties will allow you to get better, more desirable locations for your real estate investment business.

However, keeping the investment houses for monthly income is attractive also. I feel it is better to build a monthly income base rather than selling properties for quick profits. Once the house is paid for, the positive cash flow can be used to cushion other future investments. Choose your personal style of investing. You may feel that flipping properties for quick profits might be a good way to purchase other houses.

FLIPPING
PROPERTIES

Establishing a base income can be accomplished by flipping houses also. The important thing is to establish the base income. Once the base income is in place, your time could become more flexible and your investment strategies can really begin to blossom. Buying properties to repair and sell for quick profits can be just the thing that pushes your button in real estate investing.

It takes cash to create a stable base income, but in many cases not much. It may not take thousands of dollars to accomplish the purchase of an investment property. Just the down payment may be required; therefore you could control a property worth many thousands for just a few. This is called using the power of leverage. For instance, if you purchase a house that costs $100,000 using your cash to fund the entire purchase and then sell the property one month later for $110,000 your handsome profit would be $10,000 or a 10% return on investment. Not bad, but let's look at the power of leverage. If you purchase a house for $100,000 and just fund a down payment of $10,000 to buy it and sell the property for $110,000 your profit is $10,000 or a 100% return on investment. You will have only used $10,000 of your own money to control $100,000 of real estate. You can use this strategy to create your base income or use it once the base income is in place. It all boils down to having positive cash flow that funds the monthly base income. Some may choose to get cash from buying depressed properties in good areas, repairing these properties and selling them for profit a couple of months later.

I have a friend that chooses to invest this way. He likes the idea of getting the profit out of a house quickly. He pockets a little profit and reinvests the remainder. His plan is to save enough profit to establish a base income with the purchase of rentals in the future.

BEGIN YOUR SEARCH

Finding the fixer upper may be easier than you think. You will most likely find one with a real estate agent, bank, being aware of your local housing market, newspaper ad, friends and relatives, driving around various neighborhoods, job transfers or other investors cashing out.

Real Estate Agents

Find a real estate agent that will diligently search for bargain properties that can be repaired and sold. Do your own search in areas that fit your criteria. Also, determine how much you can invest and don't stop searching until you find a deal that you can profit from.

Real estate agents have listed houses not only in your city, but surrounding areas. An agent can show you houses in specific sizes and price ranges. Furthermore, this information is free to you. Allow them to work for you.

Banks

Talk to banks that have repossessions on their books. In many cases, most of the purchase price financing is handled in-house so your money remains in your pocket. Creating a professional friendship with people who work for lending institutions can be rewarding also. They can provide much help in your getting financing in the deals they have and the ones that you find.

In your search for a bargain property try to find a house that is in need of repair and is priced well below market. This might include houses that have been for sale longer than most, or a house for sale because of a divorce.

Why won't
this house sell?

Houses that have been on the market for a long time might have one obstacle preventing a sale. If you find a house that fits your investment plan and it has been for sale more than six months, learn to recognize the obstacles involved. I found a house that had been vacant for over a year. A buyer couldn't be found because of interior conditions of the property. A small section of the ceiling was falling and the floor structure was rotting in three of the six rooms. At first glance, it seemed to be in a condition that would not be worth repairing. The floor structure looked like termites had damaged it. The dreaded word "termites". I recognized this to be the reason people did not want this property. It was the very obstacle that kept potential buyers away. They didn't know how to recognize the real problem behind the rotting floors. I noticed the small area of damaged ceiling was allowing rainwater to fall on the floors. The water soaked into the wood and damaged it. It wasn't termites at all. It was just water damage. After I purchased the property at a deep discount compared to other houses in the area, two boards were repaired on the roof and the problem was remedied. The old floor joists were removed, the new ones were put into place, and plywood was laid over that. This was a small problem that looked like a huge one.

Examine repair problems and teach yourself what to look for. If it seems extensive, have the house inspected by a professional. In many cases, it is just simple problems that prevent the sale of some properties. When you find a deal like this it can be very profitable to flip it for quick profits.

Newspaper Ads

Newspaper ads are also great sources for bargain houses. Many sellers don't want to pay commissions on a $25,000 house. If you search the ads daily, eventually you will find houses to make offers on.

Friends and Relatives

Once you begin investing, friends and relatives will begin to look for and find houses for you. I bought several houses that other people found because they knew that I was investing in real estate. Put the word out for them to start looking. Instead of having your own sales force, you will have your own buying force! People love to shop, so let them help.

Drive and Search

Try to spend one or two hours a week searching for houses in neighborhoods you might be interested in. Match the neighborhood to your investment dollar. Don't look for properties where the houses sell for $90,000-$125,000 if you only have $30,000 to invest. The more effort you put forth searching for properties, the better the results will be. Your skills for finding properties will get better as time goes by. You will get a feel for prices and rents of specific areas also.

There are other creative ways of finding bargain properties, some you may even find yourself. However, these strategies are a good place to start. If you are diligent and patient a sizeable income can be built with bargain properties.

Finding a bargain property does not mean finding a house priced below $50,000. You might find a fixer upper that is priced at $150,000 or $250,000. It may be a great deal in the particular area that it is in. If you choose to invest in more expensive properties be sure to search for the bargain. The principal is still the same. In many cases these types of properties offer excellent rental income and they usually appreciate in value very quickly. Find a fixer upper in any price range that you feel comfortable with so you can build your equity and boost your monthly income and net worth. This is an opportunity for any investor that chooses to receive a monthly income or chooses to sell the property for a quick profit.

Job Transfers

At any given time there are several houses across our country listed for sale because of job transfers. Real estate agents can help in this area of investing. Many times companies want to sell quickly to finalize a deal with an employee. Businesses are more likely to take a loss on a property just to move on. Ask your agent to be on a constant lookout for these deals. You may have more time to sell the house than the company does. Therefore, these are typically good properties to flip for quick profits.

Investors Cashing Out

These could be excellent buying opportunities for beginning investors. Some people that have been investing for many years want to sell smaller investment houses and move to multi-family units or commercial properties. They look for a quick easy sale so they can move quickly to the other deal.

Try to get involved in investor groups in your area or introduce yourself to several investors wanting to do the same thing you do. Networking with friends is not only fun, but also it can be a good source for finding properties. One person cannot buy all the potential investment houses so make friends and help each other succeed.

CREATIVE SELLING

Just as there is creative financing and creative purchasing, there can also be creative selling of properties. It is your property, so sell it the way both parties can agree on. Be as creative as you need to be in order to make your purchaser feel like you have both won. There are many ways to make this happen such as accepting conventional financing for the entire purchase price, owner financing the entire purchase price, owner financing a portion of the purchase price, lease purchasing, lease purchasing with an option and bond for deed.

Conventional Financing

If you are interested in flipping properties, accepting conventional financing is usually the way to sell. You would actually sell the property and receive all of the money out of it at that time. This allows you to recoup all of the money and move on to the next property.

Owner Financing
the Entire Purchase Price

This would probably be the easiest way to sell a property. Be cautious however, because the purchaser has no money in the property at first. The seller might assume some risk by not requiring the purchaser to put money down, therefore increasing the chance of the seller having to repossess. Owner financing without requiring any money down might be a good way to sell to a family member or a good friend that you could trust. Someone that you feel certain would not devalue your property or leave you in a negative position on your monthly payment. This could be a good way to sell for both parties. Good for the buyers because of the financial ease of the purchase. Good for the seller because of the interest collected monthly on the principle and profit.

Owner Finance
a Portion of the Purchase Price

This is another creative way to sell a property. If $40,000 is invested in a property and the selling price is $70,000, one could ask $40,000 down through conventional financing and carry a second mortgage on the remaining $30,000. All of the original investment would be returned and the remaining $30,000 would be received monthly with interest attached.

Lease Purchase

Lease purchase is good for both the seller and the buyer. It is good for the buyer because of the ease of an owner finance transaction and, in many cases, less expensive to acquire ownership. It is good for the seller because the lease period provides a way for the seller to document the payment consistency of the buyer. It is good to have a lease period before a sale to reduce the possibility of having to repossess because of inconsistent monthly payments. You could either reduce the purchase price by the amount paid during the lease period or not. That is entirely up to you. The purchaser needs to be informed as to how this will be handled.

Lease With An
Option To Purchase

Lease with an option to purchase is basically the same as a lease purchase with one exception, the option money. Before the prospective purchaser moves into the property, an option to purchase payment would be paid. This serves as a down payment on the property if the tenant decides to take ownership at the end of the lease period. The lease period could be as long as both parties agree upon. The lease period and the option payment could become extra profit on the sale of the property. For instance, if your investment property cost $40,000 total including purchase and repair, the lease option payments are recouped from your original investment.

Original Investment	$40,000

Deduct the following:	
Lease Period 3 Years @ $700/mo.	$25,200
5% Option to Purchase	$ 2,000
Investment After 3 Years	$12,800

Before the property is actually sold for $60,000 to $70,000, a return of $27,200 has been recouped. When the property changes ownership the entire investment of $40,000 would be paid back in 5 years. Now an owner-financed note is being held between $60,000 and $70,000 with interest attached. This investment strategy is very profitable for the seller and it can be great for the buyer also.

Creative selling is a way to maximize your profits in investment properties and allows people to take ownership in properties that they would never have been able to any other way. Be sure to create a sale that could be good for both seller and buyer.

Bond For Deed

The seller retains actual ownership of the property until the property is paid in full. This kind of sale protects the seller because it avoids repossessions. If a buyer defaults on payments a simple eviction is required. Therefore, the seller would not have the expense of repossessing.

When purchasing properties, try targeting less expensive houses at first. Remember it is much easier to build your base income foundation with less expensive properties. The houses are paid for quicker, therefore your positive income foundation can build your business faster. This can result in a possible full-time investing career, or just extra retirement dollars. A good positive income from rentals will ease the stress of vacancies also. As I said earlier, if you accumulate three houses in your business each renting for $500 monthly and each of them are paid for, it becomes much easier to add the fourth. These three incomes will pay for the fourth. If one becomes vacant, the other houses pick up the slack. The worry is much less and your business could be on the verge of expanding quickly.

Once your base income is in place, your investment possibilities can really expand. Now that your assets are in safe investments, banks will more likely loan you money on future properties. Your properties also provide diversity. All your eggs are not in one basket. There are different eggs in every house you purchase. If one becomes vacant, others can help. If you sell one house to buy a better one, there are still other houses paying you.

Wouldn't it be great to have an income from real estate to fall back on if needed? You can have it, one house at a time. Create a plan; be patient, structured, and diligent. A real estate investing business is of your own creation. I believe most people can do this. Begin by trying to find an inexpensive property to get your feet wet. Once you get your first property paying your bank account monthly, you will begin to realize the ease of this business. Build your business with seven, ten, or fifteen houses. Then you will have a good foundation of income in place.

These are realistic short-term goals for most. Even if you don't want to do this full-time, it could pad your retirement account. The income could pay for education expenses, vehicles, and elaborate vacations in the future. The best part of this scenario is that the money isn't spent. It is saved in a property that provides a foundation of monthly income.

EVERY DIFFERENCE OF OPINION IS NOT A
DIFFERENCE OF PRINCIPLE.

THOMAS JEFFERSON

CHAPTER 3

WHAT ABOUT PURCHASING A RENTAL HOUSE?

Let's get started by determining how much money you can invest today. Look in every area of your finances. Paying for your first house is a plus, but not a must. There are a lot of ways to purchase real estate with no money down. However, I feel that it always has to be paid back so the more you can put down, the better. Unless you're flipping a property using leverage, starting your business with a lot of positive cash flow is a real asset. Your income will grow from the property, and your net assets will be greater. Investing your money in real estate assets is like a forced savings. You're not only purchasing, but also saving the money. The money is not really spent. It's just put into a property that provides income and possibly interest and can be sold at any time to get your cash back. If you choose to sell, in most cases, you are going to recoup more cash from the property than when you purchased it not to mention the rents collected in the meantime. If you have to borrow money for your first property in order to create your monthly base income, force yourself to pay it off early. No money down deals work better if you have income from other properties to fall back on to pay for the debt. Be creative in looking for extra money or income. This may include getting a part time job for six months or selling unneeded items around your house.

My first rental house was owner financed to me. Instead of getting a loan from a bank, the seller carried the note on the house. Sometimes this is a great advantage to the buyer. The steady monthly income and the interest attached to the note can be a real advantage to the seller also. Sometimes sellers don't need all the cash immediately from a property. It can be an advantage to buyers because owner finance deals are usually easier to qualify for, and the upfront cash required is usually less. This is an added plus for beginning investors. I needed just $1,500 to take ownership of my first rental house. The owner carried a note for $13,500 at 10% interest. The seller became the bank. My note was $150 per month, but the rental income was $300 monthly. This provided a positive cash flow of $150. That translates to an annual income of $1,800. My insurance and taxes were approximately $400 annually. As you can see, my original investment of $1,500 was paid back to me in just over a year. I had no money in this deal now, and someone was paying me money monthly. Very little of my time was put into this deal. It wasn't much money monthly, but it was a start.

Begin looking for your first deal. A good place to start looking is your local newspaper. Look at all the homes for sale. Owner finance deals really help you get a quick start, but consider any house if the investment dollars work for your portfolio. All owner finance deals are not good investment purchases, but some are. Look at them carefully. Some sellers are just ready to sell. That was the situation with the person that sold me my first house.

As I said earlier real estate agents are a good source for finding properties. Search for an agent that you are comfortable with. This should be someone that you know will look out for your best interest. Ask him or her to give you a list of all the houses in your price range. The area of your city or town may not be a big factor. In most cities, people live in good areas and bad. If an investment house is available in a less desirable part of town, most likely someone lives next door to the property. These houses are usually easy investment starts because of their low price. Even though some areas are not so great, they sometimes command really good rents. As I said earlier however, don't buy properties in declining or high crime areas. Find the fixer upper in older but clean communities. Neighborhoods that people are proud of. Low priced properties can help build your income fast. The faster you build your part time income, the sooner it becomes full time. Find your personal investment style.

I did not have starting capital for my real estate investing dream. I had to search for low priced properties that had potential. These low priced houses were purchased and paid for relatively quickly, therefore enabling my business to become full time. My first house was not in a good area of my city, but it has been a great investment. It has been ten years, and I am still collecting $300 monthly from it. I could probably command a higher rent, but the same renter still lives there today. I paid for the house many years ago through the refinancing of my personal home. But the initial $1,500 investment set in motion thousands of dollars of income through the years. Refinancing was one of the ways I began my quest of a real estate business. This gave me money to invest and I was able to deduct interest I paid to the bank from my income taxes. Where can you find money to invest now? Determine how much you need to invest now or possibly a year from now. Diligently search for and find the deal that matches your investment dollar. The houses are out there.

About nine years ago, I searched a neighborhood and bought a cute two bedroom, one bathroom house for $3,400. I realize these kinds of properties are few and far between and may not be possible anymore but, at the time it was a buyers market and the house needed extensive repairs. It belonged to an elderly couple that had passed on. The family did not want anything to do with the property or its contents. Many times inherited property is sold at deep discounts in comparison to the surrounding area. There are usually many items left behind because of the family's lack of interest in another person's belongings. These properties seem worthless because of the trash and debris left behind by the former owners. This was the case with the house I found. Just $500 was spent for clean up and the property seemed to be worth much more. As it turned out, it was. The house was solid and a good investment that just needed some tender loving care. The repairs included new sheetrock throughout, new cabinets, new interior and exterior doors, windows, electrical work, plumbing, and central air and heat. I had found this property in a neighborhood that matched my investment dollars. The rents in this area were about $300-$500 monthly. I thought it was a great investment. I had about $10,000 in this property and my rental income would be about $400 monthly. With a payback of less than three years, this was a perfect investment for me. It's been eight years now and I am still collecting monthly payments. I do nothing for this income. This house has paid me thousands of dollars through the years. The value of the property has also increased. I worked hard for two months and still get paid monthly and will for years into the future. It's that easy. The key is to duplicate this simple task many times.

I'm going to prove how simple it really is. Let's find, repair, and lease a house together. I cannot prove my theories to you any better than if we do it together. I want to find a simple three-bedroom house for under $20,000 in or around my city. Let's begin our search!

DAY ONE

I begin my search in neighborhoods where the houses are worth approximately $35,000 to $65,000. Two of the neighborhoods are good areas and one is not so good. I find three houses for sale by owner in the good area and two by a real estate agent in the not so good area. I call about all five. They are all in pretty good condition and all are priced above $40,000. I want to spend $20,000, so I decide to keep looking. My time spent today is about one hour.

Another way of finding bargain properties is to ask your agent about foreclosures. Banks love investors to purchase these properties from them. They are not in the business of owning houses they are in the business of loaning money. Banks might be more willing to loan money on these properties if you can show them your investment payback plan. Some banks might give you a list of these properties without an agent. My experience with repossessed properties has been very positive and profitable. Sometimes people cannot pay for their property, so they simply walk away. The houses are usually in reasonably good condition and that means less repair expense.

Let's look how just one rental property can make a difference for you. The first scenario we will look at is a fixer upper that can be purchased and repaired for $30,000 or below. In many areas of our country, I think this can be accomplished with patience, diligence, and persistence. This may be a house priced below appraisal. In this case a bank might offer full financing on the house with no out of pocket money on your part. A loan of $30,000 at 7% interest for ten years would be approximately $350 monthly. With a rental price of $600 monthly, your positive cash flow would be $250 monthly or $3,000 annually. It may be difficult to find a house for that price where you live, but the principle is still the same. If a fixer upper cost $60,000 the rents in your area might command $1,000 or more. The property would pay for itself in approximately five to seven years. This is assuming you pay no extra money to accelerate the payoff.

However, it is recommended to try to pay the loan off early. This would force you to put money away for your future. You will see that when you purchase real estate it is really like saving money, not spending it. If you ever need your cash, you can sell the property or mortgage it to get the money out of it. If you do not use any of your cash to pay the loan off early, the house will still offer you extra retirement funds. If you choose to pay off the house with extra income, you can then use the income to help purchase other properties. Let's assume a rent of $600 monthly. The first seven years of income will be used to pay off the property. Plug your age into the diagram below:

Age	Extra Retirement Funds at 65
20	$273,600
30	$201,600
40	$129,600
50	$ 57,600

These figures reflect income you will receive once the house is paid for. The property value of the house will also have increased. Adjust the figures slightly for taxes, vacancies and insurance. Remember, this is only one house and you virtually have no money in it. Renters paid for the property, not you. The rents, insurance, taxes, and various repairs will fluctuate over the time you own the property. However, they will not fluctuate enough to make the property not worth purchasing.

Let's look at a second scenario. What if you had cash to purchase this same investment property? Again, assume $600 monthly rent.

Age	Retirement Age 65
20	$324,000
30	$252,000
40	$180,000
50	$108,000

Remember, this is what one house can do to add to your retirement, a house that someone else has paid for through rents. This is a house and an income that can be passed to loved ones, be sold for quick cash, or can be used to purchase other properties.

What if you add ten properties over the next five to seven years? Could you then begin to think about early retirement? Learn to think big for yourself and your family. What about fifty properties? Would that be an acceptable income for you? It is well within your reach. Many other people just like you have done it. Why not you?

DAY TWO

Day one was a swing and a miss. It is now three days later. I have located other areas outside my city called bedroom communities. They are areas that are about 10 to 20 miles out of city limits, but are great places for families. Many times these areas offer houses that are better priced. I have found two for sale by owner houses and one by the same real estate company that offered houses in other areas I searched. I told the agent the first day that I was looking for a three-bedroom house under $20,000. The two for sale by owner houses are just overpriced. I call the real estate company about the other one. It is $33,000 and needs repairs, but he researches on his computer and finds a repossessed house for sale. The price is $18,900. It is located fifteen miles from my city in a good neighborhood. I promise him that I will look at the property in the next couple of days. I'm really not in a hurry. Today I have spent three hours on my business.

If you see the potential this business has, this might be a good time to add a couple of things to your goal sheet. These will be personal ideas and business ideas that might work for you and help you build faster. I think anyone can do this, especially just one house. The beauty of investing in real estate is that if you ever need your investment back, you can always sell the property, usually at a handsome profit. I think you will find it very rewarding. It will help you become less dependent on others and offer more financial stability in your life. Take steps to start now if real estate investing is something you are interested in. Don't talk yourself out of financial stability in the future. I've reached my goals time after time. I had to be creative and focused. You can do this too. Enjoy the financial stability waiting for you in your future. No one will do it for you. The sooner you start, the sooner it can happen. I hope some of these ideas will spark your inner drive and allow you to see the possibilities of your own real estate investing business.

KNOW YOUR OPPORTUNITY-SEIZE IT.

TENNESSEE WILLIAMS

CHAPTER 4

WHAT ABOUT BECOMING THE BANK?

I hope using my own experiences to show you how they relate to various investment ideas can work for you. My second house was a government repossession. A real estate agent found the house. Six months prior, I had mentioned to this agent that I was looking for investment houses. I'm sure she put my name on a list of potential customers and gave me a call. This house was to be sold by sealed bid. On this particular house the low bidder turned out to be me at $8,000. Eight thousand dollars! You would think there would be a lot wrong with this house. However, there really were not many problems. It turns out this was a bargain property, but it just did not look like it.

THINK OPTIMISTICALLY

It helps to be able to envision what properties can be, not just what they are now. This house was ugly! No one wanted it. Fortunately, I was able to see through the bad floors, leaky roof, broken brick, and ugly colors.

You too can see the potential in bargain properties with positive thinking. I can't stress to you enough the importance of positive thinking. If it is not a natural thing for you to think this way, teach yourself to do so. I remember when I began to think optimistically. I was friends with an individual who chose to think positively about most situations. I remember it being a very admirable trait in him, a trait that I wanted people to see in me. It didn't come naturally; it was a choice he made. You can also choose optimism for yourself. Thinking positively is not only good in a real estate investing business, but in your everyday life. I believe you can teach yourself and others around you to think positively. Sure, be a realist, but an optimistic realist. I once heard someone say, "There have been a lot of optimists that have gotten rich from a pessimist." There is a lot of merit to this phrase. It is a lot easier to do nothing and see the negative side of a situation. Many people have done this and are now working well into their retirement years. It is okay to work past retirement age if you want to, but not if you have to. It's not easy to succeed. If it were, everyone would be successful. Train yourself to see potential and to think optimistically. I let myself see the potential in this property.

The house needed central air and heat, roof repair, brick repair, and carpeting. Contractors did all of these repairs. I just coordinated the repairs. Everything else was just common sense such as light fixtures, door repair, and painting. I invested $7,000 more in the property. This made a total of $15,000. The house was in a good area, so I knew that this house was worth the investment. I think it is a good investment choice if a property can pay for itself in five to seven years. I knew this area supported monthly payment prices that ranged from $400-$700. Even if the purchase price had been double, it would still be a good investment. It doesn't take nineteen years of education to do this. It just takes ambition, intuition, and sacrifice.

TRY OWNER FINANCE

I had some cash to purchase the property and the remaining fix up cash came from a 90-day bank loan. I wanted to pay for this house quickly, because my intentions were to owner finance it. I wanted to become the bank. That way I would collect interest and principal just as the person did that sold me my first house. Another advantage to owner finance was no property taxes in my area. Insurance became the owner's responsibility, and no upkeep repair expenses. I had a bank collect payments that were deposited directly into my checking account. Once your original investment is paid back, it's like receiving free money for doing nothing.

My sale ad read like this:

Lease purchase, three-bedroom, one bath with central A/H, utility, dining, newly remodeled. Five thousand down, approximately five hundred monthly.

I could have easily rented this house as I did my first one, but this house was paid for in full. I wanted to experience an owner finance deal. The 10% interest attached to the owner finance note also intrigued me. As I said before, my total investment in this property was about $15,000. Upon completion of the lease purchase sale, I recouped $5,000. The lease period of a house can be as long as you want. The leasing period can provide you with information about the kind of payers they are going to be. Basically, the purchasers are just renting the house during this period and it becomes added profit upon the sale. I chose to lease this house for one year at $550 monthly. Another $6,600 was paid back to me in the first year. Six hundred of the first years rent went to taxes and insurance. Before the actual sale took place, I only had $4,000 in this property. The sale price was about $55,000. The note was to be approximately $500 monthly for a period of thirty years with 10% interest attached. I basically acted as the bank collecting principal and interest monthly.

Lease purchase owner financing is a great option for investors that don't want to deal with renters. If a rental business is great, an owner financing business is wonderful. Once the property is repaired, you just sit back and collect profit with interest attached to it. You actually become the bank. If you are looking for an investment opportunity to put cash into, give this a try. It should take only two or three months at the most to repair a property then you collect on it for years. The money you spend to purchase property isn't spent at all; it's saved. Try to look at it this way. If you want your money back, sell the property. You should make a profit because of the repairs and updating you have done to it. This is a very safe investment and offers a profitable return on your investment. Sacrificing two or three months of your time is not much compared to the years you can collect from the property.

If you don't have the cash to purchase a house in full, take the steps necessary to pay for it over time with a loan that doesn't require using that property for equity. Home equity loans work great for this. Getting the equity out of your personal home can be a great option for the beginning investor. The money is not doing anything, so why not create assets, income, and wealth with it. Equity loans don't always have to come from your personal home, although this is a great option for a beginning investor. Once you have houses paid for, those could then be used to extract tax-free funds from and be used to purchase others. If you choose to get money from house number one to purchase number two, then two is paid for, or nearly paid for. Then both can pay the mortgage on the first. Now the third can be added. Purchasing a house with cash from a home equity loan will allow you to sell by owner financing it. The payments from the owner-financed house can be used to pay the note on your personal home. Whether you choose a signature loan, 90-day loan, or an equity loan from another property, I would still suggest paying the loan off early so you can lease purchase owner finance. There are many ways one can create and investment plan. Think about your personal situation and create a plan that fits your way of thinking. You may be very aggressive and buy ten properties at once or a little conservative and purchase ten properties in the next ten years. Whatever your style, use the income money to reduce the mortgage on the properties. If you sacrifice and do this early, when you see your net worth building, you will look back and be glad you did.

If you choose to use the property as equity for your loan you could collect rent until the balance of the loan is paid. Once you pay your loan off, then you can sell the property and become the bank collecting interest payments.

If you decide to owner finance a property, try to set it up as a 30-year amortization. The lower payments will help the buyer, which in turn will help to sell the house quickly. The 30-year amortization will secure monthly payments for a longer period of time and your principal balance stays high longer. Your monthly income would be more with a 20-year loan, which is fine also. Do whatever is good for you and the buyer. Try to pre-qualify the buyer! Applications can be purchased at an office supply store.

You should ask for a down payment before a purchase. Banks usually ask for 20% down. I usually ask for 5%-10%. If I really like the applicant and the down payment is an issue for them, I will finance some of the down payment. You can include this in the monthly note until it is paid. Good for me because I feel comfortable with the buyer. Good for them because they are able to take ownership of the house with less money.

It took approximately two months to complete the purchase, do the repairs, and to sell this house. I did it all in my spare time. It may seem difficult to do repairs on houses, but it is mainly just coordination and common sense. The more difficult tasks such as central air and heat or roofing can be coordinated with people who do that for a living. I'm sure there are several contractors in your area that would be happy to give you prices on your project. I completed this project nine, or ten years ago, and the house still pays me $500 monthly. Do the math. It was worth the sacrifice back then to have it now.

Not bad for two months work and coordination in my spare time. If I had not done this back then, I would not have the income and asset now. I bet if you think back, you realize that time moves on pretty fast. Don't let another five years pass and then say, 'I wish I would have done that'. Look back and say, 'I'm glad I did'. You can be in control of your future starting now.

DAY 3

With a cup of coffee in hand I drive and find the house for $18,900. The house is about fifteen years old and surprisingly in good condition. Most fixer uppers need about the same repairs. This one needs central air and heat, minor cabinet repair, painting inside and out, toilet, vanity, and ceiling light fixtures. The area this house is located in supports prices of $30,000 to $70,000. Remember, I need to stay under $20,000. I estimate repairs of four to five thousand, so I offer $15,000. Time spent this day is one hour.

If this seems simple to you, it's because it is. Think

positively and creatively. Don't make this harder than it has to be. Get your first deal done! With the purchase of your first house, you will begin to see future potential income. One house is not much money monthly, but the income from seven, eight, or ten houses is. It will take some time, but persistence could turn this into a great part-time income or even a rewarding career.

DAY 4

We'll call this day four, but three days later my offer is accepted. I notice a vacant lot next to the house and wonder if it is included. At the closing three weeks later, I find out that it is. The time I have in this property from the search to purchase is about six to seven hours. When repaired this house will support a sale price of about $50,000 and the extra lot another $10,000. Seven hours work with a potential $40,000 built in profit, and we're doing it together. Now let's repair the property so we can sell or lease it.

BUY A HOUSE,
KEEP THE INCOME

Find a house that will match your investment dollars. Pay for at least one house so you can owner finance it. The power of becoming the bank is incredible. I don't believe in buying a house and cashing out the profit, until the base income is established. Once a house is purchased, it can provide monthly income. Our society requires us to live month to month. Don't buy and sell until your base income is in place. Buy and hold. If you buy and sell for cash, you have to repeat the process over and over. You will not create your monthly income base and you constantly have to find more houses. Sure, you can sell for a quick profit, but why sell a house just to go and look for another? You own this house, so why not sell it monthly with interest? Create your base income first, then buy and sell for quick profits later, using leverage.

When selling a house owner financed, you not only collect 10% interest on your original investment, you also collect 10% interest on the profit. This makes the 10% on the original investment look like pocket change. I used 10% for an example, but you can set your own rate. In most cases there is a 12% cap. One reason the interest rate is inflated somewhat above the bank is because of the risk involved. People wanting to purchase homes through owner finance may find it difficult to receive a loan from a bank. This should not scare you because buyers put cash down to purchase. They now have a vested interest in the property as well as the pride of ownership. Therefore, they are more likely to follow through with the purchase.

In many cases it is very easy to sell a house by owner financing it. You are able to help people own their own home instead of renting. The monthly note is usually less for a person buying than it is renting. Therefore, your number of potential buyers is huge. Most renters, given the choice, would rather own. Do you see the potential? It's a good deal for the buyer and the seller. You help the buyer become an owner when, otherwise, they may not have the chance. The buyer now has an asset that will grow and they have the pride of ownership. The seller receives monthly payments with no repair expenses, insurance cost, or property taxes. The seller has no worries from renters and is able to receive interest from the loan. The interest attached to the loan is the best bonus of the sale. Banks receive interest on every loan they make. Why can't you? Selling a house this way becomes a tremendous investment. For example, let's consider a house you could purchase and repair for $30,000. You choose to cash out and sell if for $60,000. Your profit would be $30,000 less Federal and state income taxes. Your profit would be approximately $20,000-25,000. That's not bad for a short-term investment, but let's look at the flip side. If you choose to owner finance this house your profit is paid to you monthly. Over the life of a 30-year mortgage, you will receive about $525 monthly at 10% interest. This calculates to $6,300 annually and about $190,000 over the term. Your original investment of $30,000 and your annual taxes are subtracted from this. However, you pay taxes only on the interest received annually, which makes the investment more attractive. The owner financed house is much more profitable and it provides monthly income. After three, five, seven, or ten years of income, you can still get cash from the property from selling the note. It doesn't take long to receive your original investment back either. Once you do, the house will still pay you monthly. It's like free money coming into your account every single month that you own this note.   Purchase a house and try this investment idea. The payments can easily be figured by purchasing an Equal Monthly Amortization book at a local bookstore.   Look at the interest rate you want to charge and the price.   Then the payment price can be matched.   A local attorney can close the sale and your bank can collect payments for you.   Now, with the purchase of rentals and the sale of owner financed houses, you are well on your way to experiencing the lifelong power of real estate investing.   Once you discover three, five, or eight houses paying you monthly, you won't stop there.

DAY 5

The   coordination   begins   with   the   air conditioning   contractor   and   the   roofing contractor.   This house had a central air and heat at one time.   The outside unit is missing and the inside unit needs changing.   The ducts are in place as well as the copper pipes.   This enables me to save money on the air and heat system. The house is about fourteen hundred square feet and requires a two-ton unit that cost a total of $1,500. The roof is about fifteen years old and is in good enough condition to lay another roof right on top of the existing one without tearing it off. This allows me to save about 50% on the roof expense. The cost of the new roof is $800 for material and $300 for labor for a total of $1,100. I just coordinate the work today. I also make a list of certain things that I could start on the inside of the house. My list includes new toilet and vanity fixtures which cost about $140, seven new interior doors which cost $45 per unit at a discount retailer, new ceiling fans with lights in all rooms which cost about $20 each at Wal-Mart, five gallons of interior paint, and five gallons of exterior paint. The paint will cost about $120. I spend about two hours today coordinating and making my list.

In my example, I am using prices from the area I live in. Prices may vary across the country, but should be relative based on income in the area. For example, property may cost more, but income and rents are also higher. It is important, however, to purchase houses in a price range that offers a rental price that targets most renters in that area. If most potential renters want houses priced at $700 monthly, purchase a house that coincides with that price. Look for a house that sells for $30,000 to $50,000 to receive $700 monthly. Of course, you wouldn't look for houses priced at $125,000 for a rental of $700 monthly. Calculate all of your expenses on the property including property taxes, insurance, repairs, and potential vacancies. Don't price your house in a way that you end up in a negative position. Purchase for the positive cash flow. Figure out where yours will be before you purchase so you can know what the house will rent for monthly and if it will support that price for that area.

THE OPTIMIST PROCLAIMS THAT WE LIVE IN THE BEST OF ALL POSSIBLE WORLDS, AND THE PESSIMIST FEARS THIS IS TRUE.

JAMES BRANCH CABELL

CHAPTER 5

WHAT ABOUT MULTI-FAMILY UNITS?

Don't limit yourself to just thinking of houses. Once you see the possibilities of investing in rental houses, multi-units can also be very good short or long-term investments. I like diversification and having both. Building a solid base income from houses or apartments can easily propel you into buying properties faster, enabling your business to become full-time faster. The key is building a base income. Remember, once again, you must sacrifice now to have later. Create a plan to pay for five to ten income- producing properties over the next five to seven years. Do this with home equity loans, with extra income, conventional loans, or 90-day loans. In some cases, 90-day loans can be stretched into three years before they must be paid in full. Remember, if you sacrifice to pay off one property, the income from that property can help pay for the next. Then two can pay for three. All the while, you are still using your income to accelerate payoffs. Once a base income is established with enough money to pay your monthly bills, the sky becomes the limit. You can also build a base income with multi-unit properties. However, it is usually easier to start with smaller properties, and a loan officer will probably have no problem taking a chance on you because of the income base that you have established in houses thus far. Sure, this is conservative thinking, but this strategy may offer less risk for the beginning investor. Be more aggressive and accelerate purchases if you choose. You might choose to exclusively deal with multi-unit properties. If this is your interest, stick to it. Find the property that fits your investment style. Devise a plan that helps you to purchase and extract residual funds monthly to expand elsewhere. Make sure the purchase price is low enough to enable you to extract funds. It is so important to use residual income from investment properties to expand. If you take the necessary steps and sacrifice the extra income for investment purposes only, you can receive real benefits from it in the future. Sure you don't know if you are going to be here in the future, but what if you are? Wouldn't it be nice to go golfing, fishing, or work on your hobby at any time you choose to do it? Build a real estate investment business one month at a time using houses or multi-units if you choose. I just personally chose to build a base income with houses because I could not get financing when I started investing ten years ago.

REAL ESTATE RISK

Establishing a base income with houses may be a conservative way to think, but it can be a time of learning. There is not a lot of risk involved in buying a house, then another, then another, until a base income is established. Small multi-family units such as a duplex or a four-unit complex can also be a good choice for success. One advantage to having multi-units is that it provides multiple incomes from one piece of property. In some cases, finding two, four, or even ten units together in one place is less expensive than if you were to buy them separately. It might be just as easy to get financing on a duplex or six-unit complex as a house. Some investors may prefer to begin with multi-units because of this.

Sometimes the positive cash flow may be so good that a payoff is not that important either. I have multi-units now that I have no intention of paying off. Yes, the note is very expensive, but I treat it as the cost of doing business. The positive cash flow is plenty to sustain the note, all expenses, and provide enough residual income to purchase other properties. Just as any base income is used to expand, residual dollars from multi-units can be used also. I have positioned my investment in multi-units to be used to purchase single-family dwellings. Most of the residual monthly money collected is used to purchase houses that can be owner financed. Once again this enables me to collect monthly principle and interest. It is basically not costing me anything to expand my business. The multi-unit facility is providing the growth of my business and it is growing in value also. If you purchase a multi-unit property it is good to get equity out whenever possible. The equity will allow you to expand your business further. But only expand until you are comfortable with your level of debt. I am very comfortable with the risk involved in my multi-family units because of the base income that I created from single-family houses. By having several houses paid for at the time, the bank was able to see my asset and income base and be more comfortable in loaning a large sum of money to a young investor. I am not saying that you shouldn't begin an investing business with multi-family units. I'm just stating the comfortable, conservative route that has worked for me. As a young man, I wanted to build an investing business one house at a time until I was financially able to purchase multi-units.

Day 6

I rent a pressure washer and a paint sprayer about 7 A.M. I spray the house with bleach and begin to wash the exterior. It takes about 2 hours to complete this job. While the exterior is drying, I replace three broken windows and change five exterior window trim boards. My nephew, who wants an extra job and who I love to work with, scrapes peeling paint while I am preparing to paint. I begin spraying at noon. It takes approximately three hours to spray five gallons of paint on the house. Once complete, we promptly return the washer and sprayer and we are now ready to finish the exterior painting the next day. This was a hard, but fun day. Time spent is 10 hours.

CASH TO SPEND?

If you are an investor with cash on hand and are looking for investment opportunities, don't reject the idea of starting with multi-family properties. These properties usually command a large purchase price. Therefore, I suggest never paying it off. Take advantage of the excess income and the increased value of the property over time. Treat the expenses as the cost of doing business, but use the excess income to expand your investments. Pay your loan off when you decide to sell the property in the future whether it is a short or long-term investment. It would be great to find a property where the note is approximately 30% of the gross monthly income. Try to purchase a multi-income property that will support itself at a 40-50% vacancy rate. With these two factors in place, there should be plenty of residual investment dollars.

Try finding multi-family units in bedroom communities around your city. The purchase price and the rents may be less expensive. This could be a win-win situation for you and the prospective tenants. Smaller towns surrounding a large city are good for an investor because of lower purchase prices. It becomes easier for an investor to buy because the risk is lowered and it's easier to secure a lesser loan amount. Look for communities people are moving into from larger cities. The rents might be less, but it's relative to the purchase price and this could mean there are plenty of prospective tenants. Many people choose to drive an extra twenty minutes to live in smaller, less expensive communities.

When the value of the property and rents increase over time it might be wise to extract tax-free funds through an equity loan. Using equity in these types of properties is an excellent way to expand. Tax-free dollars can be extracted and used for other investments. Your investment business is growing while other people are paying for it. The lump sum money can be used for personal debt reduction, purchase of other multi-family units, houses to be financed, or rentals. These new investment properties can pay for your increased note amount. "OPM". Using other people's money to pay your debt, grow your investments, and net worth. This works great for a long-term plan. Ideally we would like to have all the income from these properties without mortgage expenses, but most of us won't at first. When you mortgage properties it takes a while for them to be paid off. Eventually they will be paid or the mortgages will be bought down enough to extract profits. Take advantage of the time that will pass anyway. Five to ten years seems like a long time, but if you look back you'll realize it's not. Create a long-term plan that will allow you to become more flexible in the future. Don't deviate from your path; stick with it! Be patient in your search. I've been able to find several that fit my criteria. I haven't purchased all of them, but they are out there. If you are interested in multi-unit properties, be patient and find the one for you.

TENANT PROBLEMS

If you choose to purchase multi-family apartments, problems will surface with some units because of the number of people living in one place. It is only a wish to think everyone will get along at all times. Rectifying the situation to keep other tenants happy is the only solution. Do what you can as quickly as possible to make sure the other units are not disturbed. Vacancies are the last thing that you want, so try to do what is right and keep everyone happy.

VACANCIES

If you encounter a vacancy, make sure you offer a nice, clean apartment for a prospective tenant. If the apartment needs updating do what you can to make your units more attractive than the competitors. Adjust your price if needed. I would rather be $10 cheaper with full units than $10 more expensive and be sitting on vacancies. If you are priced a little below market, you stand a better chance at 100% occupancy. You might be worse off in the long run by expecting high priced rental rates. Three or four vacancies can be much more expensive than if you expect a little less and sustain maximum occupancy. The key is to offer a little more for a little less. You stand to maximize your income and you feel good about your prices in the process. It's a win, win situation.

IF YOU DESIRE MANY THINGS,
MANY THINGS WILL SEEM BUT A FEW.

BENJAMIN FRANKLIN

CHAPTER 6

WHAT ABOUT FIX UP AND REPAIR?

Most bargain properties will require repairs. Don't let this scare you off. As I said earlier, most major repairs can be coordinated with repairmen or contractors. You can easily do the minor repairs yourself. Whether you are male, female, young, or old, these repairs don't require a lot of expertise, just common sense. If you choose not to do the simple repairs there are plenty of people that advertise in your local paper to choose from. Get prices and coordinate. I believe in doing some repairs myself, especially the cosmetic ones. It gets me involved in the property and teaches me something about the repair of future properties.

Most houses need basically the same repairs. This usually includes central air and heat, new lighting fixtures, new flooring, painting and general repair. Some houses need a new roof. Others will need leveling. This may sound difficult, but it really is not. Local contractors can do repairs you choose not to do. Your only job in that case will be to coordinate with the contractors. However, the more you do yourself, the more money you save. These skills will improve with each house.

The first thing anyone notices about a property is its outward appearance. Painting the exterior is inexpensive and relatively easy to do. Get family and friends involved in choosing colors and giving ideas to help improve the appearance. Trim windows and shutters with contrasting colors. It is not imperative that the property has shutters, but anything that you can install on the exterior for color contrast usually is a plus. The paint surface is easily prepared by washing with bleach and some scraping may be necessary. Always try to paint the body of the house with a paint spray gun. These can be rented at an equipment rental store in your area. I'm sure there are several to choose from and it should cost less than one hundred dollars for a daily rental. Even an inexperienced person can paint a house in one day. Don't worry about over spraying on the trim and windows because the trim will be painted another color and the windows can be scraped with a window scraper. You should be able to completely change the exterior look in less than two days. Vinyl siding is very attractive in many cases. The exterior siding might be in a condition that would require extensive repair costs. In this case, vinyl could be the answer. It is a very inexpensive way to completely change and update a property. If you consider vinyl siding, contact a local vinyl contractor in your area.

Lawn cleanup and landscape trimming is also very easy. People in the surrounding area will begin to notice the changes in a property. You should start getting inquiries about the rental or the sale of the property by completing the outside first.

There are several things that you can do on inside repairs also. Get family and friends involved in this process. Their ideas may get you more profits. It is always good to have sheetrock on the interior walls. It can be painted to brighten the area. If there is paneling, it may match the décor. In that case, leave well enough alone. Be sure to put a fresh coat of semi-gloss white paint on the ceilings. Flat white can be used, but the semi-gloss adds luster and class. Contrast walls and trim if possible. It will take more time, but a couple of hundred dollars of paint can increase the value of the property by thousands. Install ceiling fans with lights where simple light fixtures were. Update the bath by changing the toilet and vanity if needed. Match the tub if possible, but leave it in place. It is very difficult to change a bathtub. If it needs updating, get it refinished by an expert in your area. A local hardware or plumbing store may have names of people who do this.

In the kitchen the cabinets may need to be painted. If they have a wood finish, rub over them with a coat of matching stain. Apply a gloss finish to complete the updating. If the countertop is outdated or damaged, it can be redone or replaced. This will probably require a cabinet professional. Paint the kitchen and bath areas. Wallpapering is very popular, but your taste may not be suitable for a renter or buyer, and it is more expensive. Make sure the windows raise and lower properly. Change individual panes if possible. It is easier and less expensive to change the panes than it is to change the entire window.

Holes in sheetrock walls can be repaired also. Local lumber stores have products designed especially for these repairs. Once the minor repairs and painting are done, you will begin to see a drastic difference in the property. Major repairs like central air and heat, roofing, floor leveling, plumbing, electrical, or interior carpentry can be coordinated while you are doing the simple things.

DAY 7

Painting the exterior trim begins today. The house is painted tan and the trim a lighter shade of the same color. Shutters are purchased and installed with screws. The shutters are painted a contrasting forest green. The over spray on the windows is scraped with a window scraper. One gallon of paint is used for the trim and one gallon for the shutters. While I paint the exterior, a contractor is installing the heat and air system. The roofing contractor also begins the overlay. I spend 8 hours today.

If you think a price is too expensive on certain repairs, get another bid from a different contractor. I once saved $2,300 on plumbing repairs just by getting another price.

Repairs on investment properties will vary from

house to house. Some will need very minor cosmetic repair, and some more extensive repairs. Most will need new flooring. One of the biggest expenses of remodeling is new flooring. Determine what to purchase by asking a flooring specialist what other homebuilders or investors are using in their properties. I would suggest shopping different flooring companies for prices and selection. Decide what's best for your property and budget. The new flooring will really change the look of the house and complete the updating.

DAY 8

With the outside nearly complete, I am able to move inside. The roof is on and the central air and heat is installed. The first repair I decide to concentrate on is the kitchen cabinets. They are painted wood, but need touch-up. I simply paint over them using a high gloss interior. I put new hinges and knobs and they totally transform the look of the kitchen. A new sink faucet is installed along with a new ceiling fan. I begin painting all of the interior ceilings. The ceiling is made up of 12X12 acoustical tile. Some are damaged and need changing, so I begin putting new ones in place. Time spent this day is 9 hours.

Reserve the big repairs for weekend days. The small things like cabinet knobs, doorknobs, ceiling fans and painting can be done in afternoons. Coordinating with contractors can be done at any time. That is mostly time on the telephone. Do it at home or work if you choose. Sacrifice these afternoons and weekends. A little time working now translates into much free time in the future. Your time and investment is well spent. I hate to keep repeating this point, but understand that you will collect for years into the future from the properties you invest in. So, to recap, don't be afraid of house repairs—big or small. You can do the little things and contractors or repairmen can do the rest.

DAY 9

With my radio playing, I finish the ceiling painting this afternoon. Time spent is four hours. Afterward my wife and I go to Wal-Mart and purchase ceiling fans, a new vanity faucet, interior and exterior doorknobs, and interior paint. Then we go to dinner to celebrate my accomplishment thus far.

Once you go through the repair process one time, it becomes much easier the next. Your ability to see the potential in a property becomes much sharper and your knowledge of dealing with contractors improves. Learn to be a good shopper and to recognize certain aspects of a neighborhood. If you see that a lot of people are installing vinyl siding to update a wood framed house, get prices to vinyl yours. A fifteen hundred square foot house can usually be done for less than $6,000. Now you don't even have to paint the exterior. Install porch railings and do some landscaping. Inexpensive updating adds tremendous value. Be creative and ask your friends to be creative with their suggestions. It's those small changes to different areas of the house that add up to a beautiful and profitable finish. Now you can be proud of what you have accomplished. With these changes to the property, your house will be desired and command a good price.

Whether you choose to owner finance, rent, or sell, your effort is rewarded by the increased value of the property. Repairs to a property take a very short time compared to the years of collected payments on it. Most investment houses will require about one to three months of repair time. You could be collecting rents or interest payments on a house by the second or third month of ownership. Receiving consistent monthly payments from an investment is a very rewarding thing. Take the time and put out the effort for a short time and collect money for a long time.

EXPERIENCE GIVES US THE TEST FIRST AND THE LESSONS LATER.

NAOMI JUDD

CHAPTER 7

WHAT ABOUT FINANCING?

Investment properties can be financed in a variety of ways. Conventional financing is available or you can use creative financing. Conventional financing is nothing more than securing the property for the loan. Banks usually loan 80% of the value of the property. Creative financing might be getting an equity loan from your personal home or from another property. It may be a ninety-day loan, an investment partner, searching for owner financing, or just selling something of value.

FORCED SAVINGS

In the case of 80% financing, you will have to pay 20% of the purchase price to take ownership. For example, on a $20,000 price, you will have to pay $4,000 down. I think it is a plus to put as much down as you can on an investment. It's a forced savings. Your money will work for you every month. Another advantage is that the house will be paid off sooner. Then all the monthly income becomes positive cash flow to help purchase other properties and build your net income quicker.

You should get the longest term possible on a loan. This will keep your notes low while buying down the mortgage and will enable you to have more positive cash flow. Make sure the loan has no pre-payment penalty. Always use the extra cash flow to buy down the mortgage. Pay for the property as soon as possible when trying to establish your base income. The base income is just that, an income, not an outflow, of most of your money collected. Sacrifice and pay for the properties in full so you can keep all of the money to cushion your bank account for future purchases. Again, once your base income is established, then move on to purchasing and flipping properties using leverage. Concentrate on building your base income first.

NO MONEY DOWN

In some instances, houses can be purchased with no money down and banks will finance the entire mortgage with no out of pocket cash. They are 100% financed. In these cases the property appraisal is usually more than the sale price. Another way to purchase with no money down would be to mortgage one property for the down payment on another, a seller financing the down payment, or even a 90-day loan for the down payment. These bargain properties can be found every day. This is when your creativity can kick in. In each case, I recommend getting the longest term available. Once again, keep the notes low, and make sure the loan has no pre-payment penalty. If the property becomes vacant for a while, it will be much easier to pay $200 monthly instead of $400. Plus you will have positive income every month. If the property is rented for $500 monthly and your note is $200, your positive cash flow will be $300. With incidental expenses like insurance and taxes, $3,000 annually can be expected. That money can be used for mortgage reduction. When enough of these properties are paid for and your extra monthly income is beginning to feel comfortable, you can then buy houses to finance luxury items that you want. If you want a new car, buy a house that will rent for $500 monthly to pay for the car. Once the car, boat, or vacation home is paid for, you still will have the income from the house. The value of the property will also have increased. Secure long-term assets to pay for short-term assets.

90-DAY LOANS

Another great way to purchase bargain properties is with 90-day loans. These can be secured with little or no closing costs. The property doesn't have to be secured for the loan, which basically frees the property of mortgage. This will allow you to owner finance the property. If you can't pay the loan off in 90 days, simply renew the loan for another 90 days. A 90-day loan can sometimes be renewed for up to three years. In this case you will be required only to pay the interest on the loan at the end of each 90-day period. You need to check with your local bank about their requirements on a 90-day loan. This can be an excellent way to purchase bargain properties. A 90-day loan will force you to pay the house off, unlike a conventional mortgage that has a payoff term of 30 years. If you choose to purchase a house for $20,000 and lease it for $550 monthly, the income in three years would be $19,800. This would just about pay for your 90-day loan. Three years is not much time to sacrifice these payments for many years of income in the future. Sacrifice now to have later. It's not spending your money, it's saving it.

USING EQUITY

Getting the equity out of a property to pay for another is a great way to purchase properties. Early in my investing, I got an equity loan from my personal home. This enabled me to purchase real estate and use the monthly income to pay my house note. Now other people were paying my house note and I was able to deduct the interest from this loan from my income taxes. The equity in my house was doing nothing for me. It was as if the money was stuffed in the walls of my house not even earning interest. I decided to use the money, not let it just sit there doing nothing. Check with a certified public accountant in your area to see if this could be an advantage for you. Use the equity in your home or from a rental property to grow your income. The note you make will be paid by the new property you purchase and then you'll have that asset helping to purchase others. Wouldn't it be great for other people to pay your house note? I think a younger person can really take advantage of this opportunity. If God is willing, time is on your side. Taking advantage of the time value of real estate can be a real plus for most. In most areas of our country, real estate is more valuable than it was ten years ago. Time will pass regardless, so we might as well take advantage of it. It's like an income snowball. If you start finding properties now, your asset snowball could be something to be proud of in five or ten years.

DAY 10

I install ceiling fans and doorknobs today. A couple of interior doors have to be replaced and I do this also. The entire house needs to match, so I make sure the interior doors are identical to the old ones. I begin painting the interior wall a soft cream color. The trim is painted gloss white to match the ceiling. Time spent this day is seven hours.

BUYING OWNER FINANCED PROPERTIES

Find an owner-financing seller. In many cases, this is a good way to start. However, you must be patient and find the right deal. If you find an attractive investment that can be purchased through owner financing, make sure you can accelerate the payoff without penalty. Also, make sure the monthly positive cash flow is adequate. Try to pay off the property within the first five to seven years. Interest rates are usually higher in owner-financed purchases; so don't let yourself get comfortable in paying monthly over the term of the loan. Once again, pay it off early. Paying for the house in full has advantages such as maximum positive cash flow, creating net worth, forced savings, and being free to do what you want with the property. Having houses paid for will enable you to owner finance the properties if you choose.

I do not want to discuss in detail the ins and outs of the many different types of loans. If you want to create a real estate investing business, you must search banks and mortgage institutions and find creative ways to get financing. Most successful investors have sought out ways to get it done. They are no different than you. You can be a real estate investor if you desire to be. Find a property, and create a plan to purchase it. Don't be discouraged because you don't think you can get financing. Banks love investors and they love real property to secure their loans. It's not like you are trying to get money for just an idea. Real estate is a tangible asset. There are many banks, mortgage brokers, and lending institutions in your area. Shop for financing just like you shopped for the property.

ASSUMABLE MORTGAGE

Property owners sometimes have mortgages on their properties that can be transferred to someone else by simply qualifying for the amount owed. This is an easy way for a seller to sell and for a buyer to buy. This can be a very attractive way to purchase if the loan has a good interest rate and term. The banker doesn't require a down payment because you are simply assuming the mortgage. However, the seller might require an equity payment. Sometimes the sellers will owner finance this payment. In this case your new property would be purchased for no money out of your pocket. Immediate income growth without your cash spent.

When you find a property you are interested in, ask the seller if the loan can be assumed. I did this and was able to purchase a four-unit apartment building. The seller wanted $20,000 cash and I assumed the original mortgage. In many cases, sellers are willing to finance their portion of the equity. This was not the case in this transaction, but if it were, the positive cash flow would still have been great even with another $20,000 note attached. I developed another good relationship with a banker, made a friendship with another investor, and in the process had a good learning experience about creative financing.

DAY 11

Today I am painting interior walls and trim. I also make a list of measurements for mini blinds. I change the toilet and vanity faucet. Time spent is about 6 hours.

When you shop for a house to purchase, remember to find neighborhoods that fit your budget. If you feel comfortable buying at $30,000, see if the neighborhood will support a selling price of $60,000. A good rule of thumb is to try and double your investment dollar. Sometimes you can get more than this, sometimes a little less. When the interest is attached to the loan, as it is for banks, the investment becomes great. Investment houses can be found in quantities in my area for $30,000. That may not be the case in your area of the country, however, as I said earlier, rents and income are usually relative to property prices.

MONEY IS LIKE AN ARM OR A LEG—USE IT OR LOSE IT.

HENRY FORD

CHAPTER 8

WHAT ABOUT REAL ESTATE VS. THE STOCK MARKET?

There have been many millions made in the stock market. There have been many fortunes lost. The same statements can be made about real estate. So let's compare the two using an investment example of $50,000.

Investing in an individual stock can be very risky as many people discovered in early 2000. Therefore, let's use a mutual fund in the example. Mutual funds are less risky because the fund is made up of many stocks. A percentage of money invested is used to purchase shares from many different companies that make up the fund therefore spreading the risk. If one company's stock goes up in the fund another might be down, ideally creating stabilization of your money. The fund might produce double-digit gains in some years and single digit gains in others. Some years may even produce negative gains, but with your research or the help of an investment professional there are funds that can be found that can conservatively produce an annual return of

10% over time. You can use the Internet to find funds that do this as well, or some that do better than 10%. For this example, a conservative figure of 10% will be used. I think over a ten-year period a minimum of 10% should be expected. Most well known funds have and will continue to offer these kind of returns. A realistic and conservative route will be taken in the real estate investing example also.

Two friends, Stan and Tim, compare their investment strategies. Stan has no interest in real estate investing. He just wants to put his money in a mutual fund and forget about it. Tim, on the other hand, has wanted to try real estate investing. Stan searched online for mutual funds that he thought would conservatively give him an annual return of 10%. He wrote down the name of ten funds and contacted an investment professional to help him decide which would be best for him in the long run. He also estimated what his investment of $50,000 would be at the end of ten years assuming a rate of 10%.

Year	Investment	Rate	Return
1	$50,000	10%	$55,000
2	$55,000	8%	$59,400
3	$59,400	6%	$62,964
4	$62,964	11%	$69,890
5	$69,890	13%	$78,986
6	$78,986	12%	$88,453
7	$88,453	10%	$97,298
8	$97,298	8%	$105,081
9	$105,081	12%	$117,691
10	$117,691	10%	$129,460

His total return in ten years would be $129,460. Stan did nothing more than park his money in a mutual fund and took advantage of the power of compounding interest. In ten years his investment increased $79,460. This is assuming the fund was tax deferred. Some may want their money to remain liquid to be able to use it at any time they choose without facing a penalty. In this case, growth is taxed annually and the investment doesn't grow as rapidly. A tax-deferred account is usually better because interest is being collected on the money that would have been used to pay the taxes. Before you invest, check with your accountant or investment professional to see which investment strategy works best for you.

Tim has been intrigued with real estate investing for about a year. He has bought a couple of books on the subject and talked to a couple of friends about the possibilities of investing in real estate. After contacting a real estate agent and researching neighborhoods around his city he found a three-bedroom one-bathroom house that totaled $50,000. Rental rates in that area were from $800-$1,100 monthly. His house would easily rent for $900.

Year	Investment	Rental	Return
1	$50,000	$900	$ 10,800
10		$900	$108,000

Tim's total return is $108,000 plus the value of the house, which has increased over a ten-year period. A conservative increase in value would be 15% bringing the house value to $57,500. This means his $50,000 investment grew to $165,500 ($57,500 + $108,000). Tim is taxed annually on his profits, but however, there is no FICA tax on real estate income and that saves him 15.2% compared to other investments.

What if Tim wanted to be a little more aggressive with his investment? After the first year he decides to get an equity loan out of the house to purchase another. He extracts $40,000 from the first house and purchases another. He finds a fixer upper for $30,000. Tim knows that the house will need painting, flooring, central air and heat, and new lighting throughout, so he estimates the repairs to be about $10,000. The house is paid for from the equity loan from the first, so he decides to owner finance the second property. The neighborhood supports sale prices from $50,000-$80,000. Tim decides to lease purchase his house for $70,000 at 10% interest for 30 years. He wants the lease period to be three years at $650 monthly. Tim gives the potential renter the option to purchase the house at the end of the three-year lease for 10% of the purchase price immediately. If for some reason the potential buyer cannot pay $7,000 to move in, he agrees to finance a portion of the option. At the end of three years he will have collected $23,400 in rent plus a $7,000 option to purchase. This gives him a total return of $30,400. Before Tim actually sells the house he owes only $9,600 on his equity loan.

The income would be $614.31 monthly. His equity loan rate from the first property would be 6 ½% on a 30 year amortization. The notes would be $252.83, which would leave him a positive cash flow of $361.48. This positive cash flow can be used to buy down the $40,000 mortgage. Over $4,000 annually will pay the $40,000 equity loan in approximately 5 years.

In our example, another house has been added which boosts Tim's net worth by $150,000. With both houses paid for, his income increases to $1514.31 monthly. As you can see, Tim can snowball his investment dollars. He can also take a portion of his money and still invest in a mutual fund and double dip his investment strategy. Both investing ideas are great. The key is turning ideas into reality.

USING REAL ESTATE AS A SAVINGS ACCOUNT

Real estate prices accelerate so rapidly in some areas that it is sometimes very profitable just to park your cash in a house instead of a bank savings account. Some investors cannot handle the stress of stock market fluctuation, but still want their investment money to earn more that 2 or 3%. In this case, a tangible asset such as an investment property may be the answer.

I have a friend that bought a house and has never rented the house, but his investment still grows with time. He purchased the house for $19,000 and it is worth about $33,000 four years later. He basically used the house as a savings vehicle. Of course, he could have had income over the past years, but he chose not to. He knows his money is safe in the investment and he knows that he could always sell or rent it if he chooses. I think it is a great idea to use a tangible real estate property for a savings vehicle. It can be used for monthly income from rentals and the money used to purchase the property grows with the increased value of the property over time.

If you wanted to expand your money over a period of time, another option would be to flip properties to enlarge your savings account. A little of your spare time could be spent finding, repairing, and selling properties which could increase the amount in your account drastically in a short time. This is an attractive alternative for people that choose not to deal with renters, but want real estate to be their primary investment vehicle.

DESTINY IS NOT A MATTER OF CHANCE, IT IS A MATTER OF CHOICE, IT IS NOT A THING TO BE WAITED FOR, IT IS A THING TO BE ACHIEVED.

WILLIAM JENNINGS BRYAN

CHAPTER 9

WHAT ABOUT COMPLICATING TO SIMPLIFY?

Most people want to simplify their lives right now. With the stress of jobs, children, school, finances it can all be quite overwhelming. Am I saying you can simplify your life immediately with a real estate investing business? No, I'm saying you must complicate to simplify. Most people have no way of simplifying their life given the path that they have chosen thus far. It seems when people get jobs they spend the majority of their income to get what they want right now. Don't we all deserve a nice car, beautiful home, nice furniture, and a boat? If we work hard, of course we do. However, you must work to pay for all the nice things that you have acquired.

I have friends that are perfectly happy with the path they have chosen, but for some this is not the case. If you find yourself searching for other opportunities, try real estate.

DAY 12

Today I am cleaning the windows inside and out and hanging mini-blinds. I start to consider flooring. Most repairs are done at this point and I begin to get inquiries about the house. I find mid-grade carpet and linoleum on clearance and I am able to purchase them at a deep discount. Depending upon the house, I will sometimes install wood flooring, but in this one I choose linoleum and carpet. I won't include my time shopping because other personal things are being accomplished and I have another nice dinner. Time spent at the house is 3 hours.

Buying a house is not spending money, it's saving it. Months and months of time does not have to be devoted to purchasing and repairing a house. As I said earlier, you can reap long-term benefits from short-term effort. There is one catch. You must complicate your life now by purchasing and repairing the properties in order to simplify your life in the future. Do you want a different job or more income? Do you want to be able to do what you want on Wednesday morning? If so, you must take steps now. As I have said throughout this book, sacrifice now to have later. Build a base income for yourself so you can call your own shots. Owning a real estate investing business may not be what you want to do long-term, but it might help you establish enough monthly income to allow you to pursue your passion. It only took a short time in my life to achieve this. You are no different than me. Anyone can do this if they choose.

JUST THE BEGINNING
OF A SUCCESS STORY

My cousin has worked most of his life living paycheck to paycheck. He has recently started investing in houses. It took him ten years to realize that he could be where other investors are now. That is not worrying about a monthly income, not worrying about punching a time clock, not worrying about lay-offs or about whether they can afford to buy the things their family wants. I am proud to say that he has seen the light. We worked together on his first house every afternoon for about two or three hours for exactly one month. The repairs on this house were like most. It required painting, new appliances, new flooring, and repairing the central air/heat. He purchased and repaired the house for a total of $45,000. The appraisal came back at $95,000. He went back to the bank and got $30,000 tax free from the property through an equity loan. His bank note is approximately $500 monthly and he charges $675 in rent. This leaves only $175 positive cash flow, but he chose to invest the $30,000 into two other houses. One was purchased for $10,000 found by a real estate agent. He recently purchased a house for $10,000! A little more work needed to be put into this property, but we estimated the repair time to be about two months. Just like most houses, it needed a new roof, new flooring, painting, new central air and heat, and new windows and doors. We estimated the cost of repairs to be about $10,000. The house will support a rent of $500 monthly or an owner finance sale of $60,000. The ten thousand left over from the $30,000 will be used to purchase another house. This house will cost about the same as his second one. He will finance about $12,000 and use $8,000 of his cash. The third house will be a duplicate of his second. The repairs might be different, but the prices and rent will be close to the same. This house will give him a great positive cash flow that will be used to pay off the $12,000. Now he will have two houses paid for with over $100,000 in assets that will pay him around $1,175 per month. He also has the option of selling the first house for $95,000, paying off his debt, and purchase another house with the profit. Within four months he had accumulated $675 of extra income not to mention the income from the third house. With all three houses, he will collect about $14,000 annually and has worked a very short time for it. This is a good annual raise for him. He now hates that he didn't complicate ten years ago so he could simplify now. The beauty of a real estate investing business is that it's not too late to create income. He is only thirty-eight and has plenty of time to accomplish his dreams.

I have a friend named Andy who is a full time investor at the age of seventy-three. He loves keeping himself young by purchasing, repairing, and selling. His monthly income is already established so he just flips the properties for profit. His life is simplified. He is doing exactly what he wants.

Picture yourself ten years from now. What do you see if you change nothing? What could you accomplish if you start investing now? I just bet in ten years your income would be greater, your time working would be less, and your net worth would be something to be proud of. Your net worth is what you own minus what you owe. If you decide to purchase properties now, there will most likely be debt that you owe on them now. But if you take advantage of the time value of real estate, your debt would be paid down in the future. Therefore, the property value, your net worth, and your equity would be greater. This has been done a countless number of times by people just like you and me. They took a chance on their future and are winning. They are retiring early or are retiring with more than just a pension.

Sacrifice your time now and start taking the necessary steps. No one is going to knock on your door and say, 'here's a monthly income.' Make it happen for yourself whether it's one house at a time or multi-family units. Build an asset base and income you can rely on to finally start doing exactly what you want to do in life.

DAY 13

It is time for the floors. I hire a flooring installer to complete the house repairs. The process takes him all day, but I spend my time just wrapping things up. This takes about two hours. The next day I vacuum the carpet remnants and install quarter round trim around the edges of the linoleum. Time spent is four hours. The house is now complete and ready to lease or sell.

OUR EXAMPLE
PROPERTY COMPLETED

Searching, finding, buying, repairing, and leasing this property was enjoyable and it took about 60 hours of my time. It all adds up to one week of hard work for years of monthly income. I will lease this property for $425 monthly for three years, then owner finance it for 30 years. The sale price will be about $50,000 at 10% interest. The buyers note will be about $440. This money will be deposited into my account monthly. The buyer now takes ownership instead of renting. I get a great return on investment. It's win-win for everyone.

Whether you choose multi-units, single family rentals or owner financed properties, it's hard to beat a consistent return on investment like this, even if you don't have cash to invest in properties immediately. You can purchase, repair, and lease now and owner finance later. As you have seen, it was easy and enjoyable finding and repairing a property. Wouldn't it be great to have income from a few houses to rely on even if you decide to remain in your current job? This is a very profitable business and a legitimate opportunity for people who are looking to create a real estate investing business. Your new business should be fun, not stressful, so begin devoting time to this money- making opportunity.

LUCK IS NOT SOMETHING YOU CAN MENTION IN THE PRESENCE OF SELF-MADE MEN.

E.B. WHITE

REAL ESTATE RECIPE FOR THE BEGINNING INVESTOR

A lot of optimism and belief that you can do this.
A lot of perseverance to find a house and get financing.

You must spend:

1 Hour	Evaluating your current financial situation. Find out how much you can invest today.
1 Hour	Determining where you want to be and writing it down.
1 Hour	Contacting a real estate agent. Try finding an agent you like and who is very knowledgeable about your local market. The realtor association can give you a list of the top producing agents.
30 Minutes	Searching for houses in your local paper.
2 Hours	Researching houses that the agent or you have found. Also get a feel for the specific neighborhoods

that match your investment dollar. You might discover a house that is for sale by owner that is not advertised.

30 Minutes	Making an offer on a house that has potential.
30 Minutes	Closing the deal at the attorney's office.
1 Hour	Making a list of things to be done to your new investment.
2 Hours	Per day in the afternoons doing repairs to the house or coordinating repairs that you cannot do.
8 Hours	On your weekends until the house is complete.
3 Hours	Showing your property to qualified purchasers and renters.

The reward of mixing these things together is monthly income that could last as long as you would like. Repeat this recipe as much as possible. Sacrifice now so you can have later.

WE HAVE TO DO WITH THE PAST ONLY
AS WE CAN MAKE IT USEFUL TO THE
PRESENT AND THE FUTURE.

FREDERICK DOUGLASS

CHAPTER 10

WHAT ABOUT QUESTIONS AND CONCERNS?

Here are a few questions that I get asked frequently. I hope these questions and answers can help you in your quest to start investing in real estate.

How do you find properties priced below thirty thousand dollars?

It's easier than you think. Most people don't hear of these deals because investors like me are out there purchasing them. Determine an investment price range. Ask a real estate agent to search for all properties in this price range in all areas of your city. Thirty thousand dollars may not be a realistic possibility where you live. If not, target inexpensive properties that are available in your area. The principal is still the same. Good rents and profits can still be extracted from bargain properties regardless of your location. Smaller bedroom communities around your city sometimes offer excellent deals. Try to find an agent that specializes in bank or government repossessions. You can also do your own search at bargin.com or on web sites that specialize in properties in your area. Real estate companies will e-mail location and prices of investment houses.

Drive in neighborhoods that fit your investment dollar. You'll be surprised at what you can find. Many properties are sold by the owner and never get advertised. "There is gold in them there hills", you just have to go get it.

Put the word out that you are searching for a property. A friend's mothers cousin might have a house in their family that is no longer needed. Word of mouth is a powerful investment tool.

There are banks in your area that will give you their repossession list. Ask for the REO list. This is a list of repossessions and property the bank has in its possession and would love to get off of their books. Ask any bank employee and they will point you in the right direction. Don't be shy about asking. If your bank has none, try another. As I said earlier, the $30,000 house might not be possible in some areas of the country, but the rent that could be collected from more expensive properties is relative to the income of that area. The principle is still the same.

Should I use my cash
to purchase properties?

Well, I could easily contradict myself now. In my opinion, and my opinion only, I think you should spend your cash to build your base income. Having properties paid for enables you to extract the most monthly income possible without having to use your cash flow for mortgage expenses. This cash flow could be used to pay your monthly household bills. This could possibly allow you to become a full-time investor. Once your base income is in place, it would be a good time to flip properties. I would use as little of my own cash as possible and take advantage of leverage. Use the banks money not yours to flip investment properties.

Is it better to purchase and sell
for a quick profit, or purchase and hold
or the monthly income?

I've tried both. I love the idea of having a stable monthly income. Buying a property and holding it for monthly income provides security, stability, and an ongoing asset base. The profits from a purchase can be much greater because of the longevity of the investment. However, in order for some investors to get to this point, it might be better to flip a couple of properties for quick profits. The profits can then be used to purchase the long-term investments. I feel it's more important to establish a monthly income base. Once the income base is in place, buying and selling for a quick profit is a great investment strategy.

Should a house be rented or owner financed?

Both. Rent the house for a period of time. Even if the house is paid for and you have the option to owner finance. A rental agreement will allow you to get a payment record of the tenants. If their payments are erratic, you may not want to owner finance. Renting the house for a time will also add to the profit of the house. With the rental and the down payment, your original investment could be returned before you ever finance it.

You can take advantage of depreciation of a rental unit and there is no FICA tax involved on real estate income. That is a 15.2% advantage of real estate investing versus other investments. If you have a mortgage on the property, rent it until the mortgage is paid. If you decide to hold ownership, keep renting.

A great advantage of owner financing is the interest attached to the note. Not only are you making interest on your original investment, but on the profit as well. This is a powerful monthly income and asset wealth builder.

Rent or owner finance-it's your call. Create the investment style that fits you best. The important thing is that you do it. Build your income, so you can be free to choose.

What if the tenant pays late?

From time to time this will happen. That's why it is so important to have several properties paying to help cushion these times. There will be legitimate reasons tenants don't pay on time. The loss of a job or an illness might be possibilities. I think it is good for an owner to be sympathetic when possible. However, some tenants will try to use excuses too often. I think you will know the difference between someone really needing help or if someone is taking advantage of your kindness. Don't let late payments become a habit for tenants. Most pay on time because they need a place to live. Moving from place to place becomes very expensive. If a tenant gets in a financial bind, it is okay to work with them from time to time. Your rent might be late, but most of the time it will be paid in that same month. I feel that it is better to work with the tenant than to have vacancies.

Should an owner
charge late fees?

This is at your discretion. You are the owner, so you set the rules. I think it is good to have a late fee policy in place just to deter a late payment situation.

Should owners
charge deposits?

Always! A customary charge is usually the same amount or close to the monthly payment amount. If there are damages, they are not typically more than the deposit amount. If there are no damages at the end of the lease period and the apartment or house meets your cleanliness guidelines, then return their deposit in full.

Should an owner finance
or sell bond for deed?

There are advantages to both. When the seller is financing the ownership is transferred to the buyer. The buyer is responsible for taxes and insurance. The seller retains ownership with bond for deed until the property is paid for. The seller is responsible for taxes, insurance, and liability. A simple eviction notice is usually required if a buyer defaults. With an owner finance contract, a repossession usually must take place if a buyer defaults.

What if I know nothing about repairs?

There will always be someone who does. Most repairs are common sense, but if you don't know how to repair something, find someone who does. People found in your local newspaper or yellow pages can do specialized repairs such as air conditioner/heat, roofing, plumbing, electrical, and flooring. Be sure to get two or three prices just to know that you are getting the best deal possible. Establish a relationship with the people you choose to work with because they could help you on future projects. They are usually more willing to work with you if they know you will have work for them in the future.

What if my spouse is not as excited about investing as me?

I suggest writing your investment plans on paper to show the possibilities of real estate investing. My wife was very afraid of my first steps, but realized in a short time what it could do for our future. Teach your partner about saving money in an investment instead of spending it for the investment.

I have a friend that did not start investing until he retired from his job as a deputy sheriff. Even though his pension was about $1,000 per month, he still found a way to begin his investing journey. His spouse was very afraid of spending their last dollar for a rental house. I am sure she is happy now because they are multi-millionaires through the process of real estate investing. He saw an opportunity and had the desire to make it happen, even after retirement. Tell your partner about success stories and about how it could become possible for you to do the same. Get them involved in the process of creating income.

What if I find a house that is priced above $100,000?

This might seem like a lot of money to purchase a

rental, but in many areas of our country it is not. Houses that sell for $100,000 or $120,000 might have an appraisal value at $150,000 to $170,000. Use leverage to purchase these types of properties, and use as little of your own money as possible. A few repairs can turn these kinds of properties into good deals. Keep in mind that the basic investment strategy is still the same. If you choose to purchase any house, but especially one with a higher price, make sure the rents cover all expenses and possible vacancies. The last thing you want to happen is having an investment property that puts you in a financial crunch. The object is having other people pay for your investments. Houses that cost more usually appreciate in value quicker than lower priced houses and are usually rented by very stable tenants.

In some cases, it is good to purchase a house and live in it for a couple of years, only to buy another and do the same, each time renting the previous house. Over time your equity will grow and your mortgage will be lowered. This is a good way for beginning investors to start a long-term rental business that could build wealth for their future.

Should I use equity

from my personal home?

In my opinion, yes! Equity in your personal home can be used to grow your income and wealth. Use the money to purchase investment properties that will pay the increase in your mortgage payment. In many cases, the entire mortgage payment can be paid by the new investment. The interest deduction is another advantage of using home equity loans.

Should I use equity
from other rentals?

Yes, to a certain extent. I would not suggest mortgaging everything you own. Your main goal should be to have positive cash flow from your properties, although in the early stage of your business, equity loans area a quick way to expand. As your income level increases over time, your debt should begin to decrease. You must be comfortable with your level of debt, so find your personal comfort zone and don't deviate from it.

Should I search for bargains
in certain areas of my city?

Yes. When doing your own search, try to find a house in neighborhoods that you are interested in. Research the selling prices and rents of the area and find the bargain priced well below market. When an agent is doing a search for you make sure the area fits your investment criteria. Also, an agent can really help you with this step because of their access to price ranges in various areas. They can provide you with informal appraisals called CMA's.

Should the property
be inspected before purchase?

Always. If you are not qualified to recognize and estimate the amount of repairs, contact a home inspection service to help you. Most repairs are very easy to recognize and this becomes easier with each house. However, some damages are hidden such as termites. Get experienced in this area. Knowing your repair costs up front will help you to know the price to offer for properties. With this information you can estimate your profit before purchase.

What about helping tenants
with their rental payments until
they can get back on their feet?

If you can help someone who truly needs it, you will feel great and be rewarded for it in the future. You'll know the difference between someone trying to take advantage of your kindness and someone struggling with children to clothe. Wouldn't it be great to be in a position to lend a helping hand?

Position yourself! You have taken the first easy step; so don't stop the progress of controlling your future.

ALWAYS DO RIGHT.   THIS WILL GRATIFY SOME PEOPLE AND ASTONISH THE REST.

MARK TWAIN

GOALS

Know where you've been! Know where you are! Know where you want to be!

Use this as a reference guide throughout the years. Feel free to add to your goal sheet as your investment strategies change over time.   Always reward yourself for every goal accomplished. As you see your future unfolding the way you want it to, it may become a reward in itself.

GOALS FOR MY FIRST YEAR

FIRST YEAR ACCOMPLISHMENTS

GOALS FOR MY SECOND YEAR

SECOND YEAR ACCOMPLISHMENTS

GOALS FOR MY THIRD YEAR

THIRD YEAR ACCOMPLISHMENTS

GOALS FOR MY FOURTH YEAR

FOURTH YEAR ACCOMPLISHMENTS

GOALS FOR MY FIFTH YEAR

FIFTH YEAR ACCOMPLISHMENTS

About the Author

Karl Caswell began investing ten years ago in small town American and has turned his part-time income into a rewarding career. Real estate investing has given him ample free time, which he spends with his family and friends.